the art of group talk

HOW TO LEAD BETTER CONVERSATIONS WITH TEENAGE GUYS

**"Guys, I just love [deep voice crack]
this group."**
RILEY, 8TH GRADE

———

**"Hey, thanks for leading our group . . .
even though I never listened to you."**
JEFF, 8TH GRADE

———

**"Why do you want to lead our group?
Do you not have a life?"**
SCOTT, 9TH GRADE

———

**"If I decide to get baptized,
can I take my shirt off so
everyone can see my muscles?"**
CHAD, 10TH GRADE

———

"I can really relate to King David because he liked women and I really like women too."

MATT, 12TH GRADE

"Why did the Apostle Paul want to remain single? That seems dumb to me."

GAVIN, 11TH GRADE

"I don't understand how Josiah was 8 years old and became king. I'm 12 years old and I don't even know how to make my bed."

PETER, 6TH GRADE

"The last time I had to ask someone for forgiveness was when I carved my name into the side of my dad's car with a shovel."

JACE, 11TH GRADE

The Art of Group Talk: Teen Guys
Published by Orange, a division of The reThink Group, Inc.
5870 Charlotte Lane, Suite 300
Cumming, GA 30040 U.S.A.

The Orange logo is a registered trademark of The reThink Group, Inc.

All Scripture quotations, unless otherwise noted, are taken from the *Holy Bible, New International Version®. NIV®.* Copyright © 1973, 1978, 1984 by International Bible Society. Used by permission of Zondervan.

Other Orange products are available online and direct from the publisher. Visit our website at www.ThinkOrange.com for more resources like these.

ISBN: 978-1-63570-080-0

©2018 The reThink Group, Inc.

Writers: Jeremy Zach, Tom Shefchunas, Brett Talley
Lead Editor: Afton Phillips
Lead Small Editing Team: Mike Jefferies, CJ Palmer, Ben Nunes, Steph Whitacre
Art Direction: Ryan Boon
Project Manager: Nate Brandt
Design: FiveStone

Printed in the United States of America
Second Edition 2017

3 4 5 6 7 8 9 10 11 12

09/03/18

Table
of
Contents

Foreword

This is a book about how to have better conversations with teenage guys.

Because, as a small group leader, you lead a conversation with teenage guys every single week. Conversations about . . .
their lives.
their dreams.
their friends.
their more-than-friends.
and their *definitely*-not friends.

And sometimes, you even manage to lead conversations about faith.

This is a book to remind you that your small group conversations—even the ones that don't go exactly as planned—**really matter.**

But there are a few ways to make your conversations **matter even more.**

create a
safe place

**clarify their
faith as
they grow**

Introduction

You probably signed up to be a small group leader (or SGL for short) because you wanted . . .
to make a big difference.
to change the world.
to invest in a few teenage guys so you could help them develop a lifelong, authentic kind of faith.

We call that **leading small.**

Maybe you didn't know *exactly* what you were getting into when you signed up to be an SGL, but you probably at least knew this:

Leading a small group means leading a weekly small group conversation.

Kind of obvious, right?

But the truth is that figuring out how to lead a conversation isn't always obvious. It's not even easy to lead a conversation with adults sometimes. So, throw in a group of teenage guys, their hormones, their partially developed brains, and did we mention their hormones, and it becomes even more challenging.

I (Brett) have learned this the hard way (maybe even a few times) as I've led groups through the years. Each time I would begin leading a group, I had some pretty big expectations for how those weekly small group conversations should look and the immediate impact they would bring to the lives of my few. For some reason, I thought they would walk into group with the same hopes and assumptions as me, ready to open up, to share our lives in true community, to ask the hard questions they'd been wrestling with, and to have long and meaningful conversations about who God is and what that means for us each week. (Spoiler alert: That never happened. At least not at the beginning of the groups.)

Before I became an SGL, I expected to lead small group conversations where every guy . . .
paid attention.
participated.
opened up.
came prepared.
listened to one another when someone did share.
asked deep theological questions.
decided to devote themselves to full-time ministry.
and read the Bible every day just because they wanted to.

But it never failed: our group would start our time together and, well, you can guess how close they got to meeting my expectations. I would be so excited to guide this group to where God was leading us. I had a path I wanted to take them down, but it was almost as if I was trying to get us there in a church van from 1974 that had a busted axle, that's alignment was off, and was minutes away from a total breakdown.

If you've been an SGL for more than five minutes, then you already know what I've learned—that leading a conversation with a group of teenage guys doesn't always live up to your expectations. (Especially if your expectations look anything like mine did.)

If you have any SGL experience whatsoever, it's probably safe to say that **you know what it's like to have a small group conversation totally bomb.**

Maybe you led a small group where your guys weren't exactly talkative. You tried to get the conversation moving, but you were met with . . .
the sound of crickets.
blank stares.
elbows to their neighbor who won't stop flicking their ear each time you look away.

Or maybe they were a little too talkative.

Maybe you had to scream the discussion questions at the top of your lungs while they . . .
fight to be the seventh person on a couch meant for three.
watch a viral YouTube video.
argue about whose team is better, which teacher is the meanest, and whose parents have the strictest rules.

Or maybe they were just the right amount of talkative, but you're convinced that your volunteer training didn't prepare you for the kinds of topics they wanted to talk about.

When leading a small group of teenage guys, sometimes you have to beg, convince, bribe, trick or plea for them to say something—*anything*.

Other times, you wish they would all instantly get laryngitis at the same time.

And more often than you'd like, you probably head home after a particularly challenging small group and wonder,
"Did I say the right thing?
Were they even listening?
Do these conversations matter at all?"

If you've ever been there, you're not alone. Everyone who has ever led a small group of teenage guys has, at some point, wondered if they were completely wasting their time. (We don't exactly have the statistical data to support this claim, but we're pretty sure it's true.)

Especially on days when your group spends more time talking about the latest Air Jordans to hit the market than engaging in a conversation about faith, those questions are understandable.

But the next time a conversation goes completely off the rails and you're wondering if you're a terrible small group leader (or if leading a small group of teenage guys should be classified as a new form of torture), there are two things we hope you'll remember.

Here's the first:

Your small group conversations matter.

And we don't just mean those once-in-a-lifetime conversations where everyone everyone looks at the ground, pretending not to cry. We mean every small group conversation.

The one with way too many awkward silences? It mattered.
The one where you didn't get through a single discussion question? It mattered.
The one where your group wanted to know if God could make a mozzarella stick so hot that even He couldn't eat it? It mattered.
The one with more farts than words? It stunk, but it still mattered.
And the conversation you're about to lead this week? Yep. It's going to matter too.

The good news for SGLs like you and me is that the quality and effectiveness of the conversation you'll lead this week won't determine your ultimate success or failure as a small group leader. Sometimes a conversation will bomb, and that's okay because that one conversation isn't the only conversation you'll ever have with your few (by "your few", we mean your small group).

In the book *Lead Small*, we talked about the importance of showing up predictably—weekly, in fact—for your few. Actually, it's the very first thing we talked about. That's because showing up predictably, consistently, and regularly in the lives of the teenage guys you lead is the foundation of leading your small group (and of leading a small group conversation).

You may not even remember the conversations you had with your few that become so influential in their lives. I (Brett) led a group of middle school guys for three years. It was, like most middle school groups, a group of guys who were somewhat disrespectful and highly distracted. One random Wednesday night, I got an email from Andrew who was almost ready to graduate eighth grade. He thanked me for having a conversation with him way back in his sixth grade year about how God can be all loving in a very broken world. Immediately I assumed Andrew's email got hacked or his mom made him email me. But later I found out Andrew did this all on his own initiative. I didn't even remember that conversation we had in sixth grade. All I remember about Andrew that year was how he and his friends lit a sparkler in their cabin during the winter retreat and almost burned the place down.

When you show up predictably, you begin to understand that one conversation doesn't determine your success as a small group leader. Your success is actually determined by every small group conversation you've ever had, added up and then multiplied by factors we haven't yet identified. When you combine the dozens, or hundreds, or thousands of conversations you've had with your small group, they equal something pretty significant. They equal . . .

Relationships.
Trust.
Influence.

I (Shef) remember getting an invitation to a graduation party for one of my former middle school guys. It was nice to see I was invited as I hadn't really been in contact with him since he had gone to high school. His dad wasn't in the picture, so he lived with his sister and his mom. His mom knew how important it was for him to maintain quality relationships with Christian men as he grew up, and I was honored to be included in that group. I simply had to go. When I arrived I was happy to see his elementary SGL and his high school SGL. As I stood there with the SGLs from his life, I realized just how important our job was to this guy. He started as a name on a roster. We got to know each other through hours of hanging out over the years. Many of those hours could have seemed unimportant in the moment. But, it was clear on this day all of those hours counted.

I know there were weeks during this student's middle school years that I felt like our small group time was a flop. But I kept showing up, and so did my few, and this consistency created relationships that outweighed a week or two of less-than-dynamic conversations. If you walk out of group this week questioning if you said anything that mattered, relax.

Your small group conversations matter—even the ones that are difficult, frustrating, or the ones that don't exactly go according to plan. They matter because each of those weekly small group conversations are part of something bigger.

So next time a small group conversation doesn't *quite* meet your expectations, remember: **your small group conversations matter—maybe more than you think.**

But here's the second thing we hope you remember:

Your small group conversations can matter more.

In fact, that's what this book is all about—practical ideas and strategies to help you make the most of your conversations with your small group.

While the one conversation you lead this week will not determine your success as a small group leader, it will affect it. The influence you're building through your weekly conversations is important, but if you never actually use that influence to help your few build a more authentic faith, then you'll have missed it.

But you're not going to miss it. We know that because you're reading a book about how to make your small group conversations matter more, and that's a pretty good sign. You're already on your way to leading better conversations—conversations where the guys in your group will not only be able to engage, but will be able to . . .
be themselves.
share their doubts.
ask tough questions.
share their struggles.

It isn't always easy to lead those kinds of conversations, though. So if you've ever looked at your small group of teenage guys and wished you knew . . .
what to say
what not to say
what to ask
how to ask it
when to speak
when to listen
how to make them talk
how to make them stop talking
. . . then keep reading.

We don't know everything about leading conversations for teenage guys, but we've spent a lot of time leading small groups, leading small group leaders, and learning the art of group talk. And now we want to take the things we've learned and share them with you. Things we hope will help you make the most of your limited opportunities to lead a conversation with your small group.

So remember.

Your small group conversations matter. They matter because, with every conversation you lead, you're building influence, trust, and a relationship with your few that has the potential to influence them for a lifetime.

But your small group conversations can matter more. And here's how . . .

1

chapter one
prepare

Prepare

Picture this.

It's Wednesday evening. You only got half as much work done as you planned. Your lunch meeting required you to talk so much, you couldn't eat your food. You're starving.

Then you remember that tonight is small group. So instead of heading home, you . . .
race to a drive thru,
scarf down a bacon cheeseburger,
drop by the house to let your dog out,
screech into the parking lot right on time,
greet Braydon, Brandon and Brendon as they walk in (and try to remember which is which),
and catch up with your few.

Before you know it, it's time to get started, all eyes are on you and you realize you have no idea what we're talking about tonight.

Ever been there? We sure have. Now, don't get us wrong. We love our small groups. We care about them. We're committed to them. We want to have great conversations together. But . . . well, we're not always as prepared for our conversations as we should be.

If we're honest, we've all had weeks like that. It happens. If you've been with your group for some time, they might not have even noticed how much you were winging it. But on your way home, you might have wondered, "What kind of conversation could we have had if I'd been just a little more prepared?"

If you want to get serious about making your conversations with your few matter more (and we know you do), then we've got to talk about **preparation** because the first step in leading a better small group conversation is to . . .

PREPARE

We know. We know!

You're a volunteer. You don't get paid to lead a small group. You've inserted yourself into the turbulant lives of a few teenage guys, and you're going to get absolutely nothing in return, except maybe a free T-shirt and some sub-standard pizza. You're already giving a *ton* of your time by showing up and leading these conversations, and now we're suggesting you spend more time *preparing* for those conversations?

Well, yes. But it's simple. We promise!

There are three things you can do to prepare for your small group conversations each week. And you can do them all from your couch.

If you want to prepare for your small group conversation, READ your email (and not on your phone driving to group).

We know that email is outdated. (That's why we created the Lead Small app.*) That's what our small groups tell us anyway. But we're not teenage guys. We're grown ups. So, we should probably still be checking—and reading— our emails.

---

* *Find out more at LeadSmall.org.*

We don't mean those emails about buy-one-get-one jeans or free shipping this weekend. Those emails probably won't help you prepare for your small group (although you should probably bookmark them just in case).

We're talking about the weekly communication—via email, the Lead Small app, a Facebook group, or a carrier pigeon—from your student pastor.

We may not know your student pastor, but we're going to assume a few things about what they do every week. We're guessing your student pastor or youth director or coach . . .
cares about your small group conversation.
thinks about your small group conversation.
has a plan for your small group conversation.
sends you the plan for your small group conversation.

Hopefully, that communication from your student pastor tells you important information like **what *they'll* be teaching and what you'll be asking** when you get to small group each week.

Ring any bells?
No?
Then you probably need to update your contact information in the church database or check your Recently Deleted folder. Or very humbly ask someone for that info on how to download that app again and get connected to your church.

But if you've checked, and double checked, and are absolutely positive your student pastor doesn't communicate with you weekly, try not to be too hard on them. We're sure they really want you to succeed as a small group leader! So don't get mad. If your student pastor doesn't send you a weekly email, try this . . .

1. Open your email app.
2. Write a new message to your student pastor.

3. Say something like this:

Hey _____! You know what would be really awesome? I would love to get an email every week— maybe a few days in advance—that helps me get ready for my small group. My guys are crazy, and I think my small group conversations could be a lot better if I had a little time to **think about what we're teaching and read my small group questions** before I get to small group. What do you think? Thanks for everything you do. You're awesome!

Pretty simple, right?

And if your student pastor already sends you weekly updates, then your job is even easier:

1. Open your email, app, or window (for the carrier pigeon).
2. Read it.

If you already do this, way to go! You are a very prepared SGL. And hey, here's a thought: If you love getting those emails in advance, take a second to hit "Reply" to your student pastor's weekly email and say, "Thanks for sending this!" They'll love to hear their weekly emails aren't disappearing into inbox oblivion.

If you want this week's small group conversation to matter more, then you need to know what the small group conversation will be about—you know, before you walk in the door.

**Prepare for your small group conversation.
READ YOUR EMAIL.**

If you want to prepare for your small group conversation, REHEARSE what you'll say.

Have you ever had an **imaginary conversation?**
Sure you have. Maybe it was when you were . . .
getting ready for a first date or a first date in a long time.
preparing for a tough conversation with your boss.
thinking of a killer comeback to win that battle of the wits
at work.

Having imaginary conversations simply means mentally
rehearsing what you're going to say before you say it.
Imaginary conversations are helpful when you're preparing
for a date, and they're also helpful when you're preparing
for your not-so-imaginary small group conversations, too.

We're not saying you should memorize lines or write a
monologue for your small group conversation. In fact,
please don't. That's weird. **We're just saying that what
you say can probably be said better if you rehearse
what you're going to say (or not say)** *before* **you say it.**

Just like . . .
a teacher practices before taking on a classroom
of students
a pitcher warms up before his call from the bullpen
a professional musician practices before the big show
. . . you should **practice for your small
group conversation.**

As an SGL, having an imaginary conversation means trying
to anticipate how your small group conversation will go
before small group so you're less likely to be caught off-
guard during small group.

So how do you do that? Well, once you've read your email
from your student pastor, ask yourself a few questions
about **what they'll be teaching, like . . .**

- What do my guys know, think or feel about this topic?
- How does this topic relate to specific situations in their
  lives right now?

- Could this topic raise any challenging questions or strong opinions?
- How will _____ respond or feel when we talk about this?

Next, take a look at your small group questions for the week, and ask yourself a few questions **about what you'll be discussing** like . . .

- Will these small group questions make sense to them?
- How are my guys going to answer these questions?
- Will they feel comfortable answering them honestly?
- Do I need to rephrase any of these questions for my group?
- Is there anyone in my group I need to connect with before we have this conversation?

See? It's simple, but it's so important!

When you have a weekly imaginary conversation with yourself, you'll be able to better . . .
clarify your thoughts.
refine your words.
anticipate their responses.
lead the conversation.

Remember, if you want this week's small group conversation to matter more, you want to think about how the conversation will go *before* the conversation begins.

Prepare for your small group conversation.
REHEARSE WHAT YOU'LL SAY.

If you want to prepare for your small group conversation, PACK a survival kit.

No, we don't mean bandages and disinfectant (although, with teenagers, that's actually not a bad idea).

We mean the kind of supplies that will help you rescue your
small group conversation in the event of
emergencies like . . .
out of control extroverts.
awkward silences.
irrelevant rabbit trails.
general chaos.

 We'll talk about how to use these supplies
later in this book. **Just look for this symbol.**
For now, just trust us. You'll need:

- A stack of icebreaker questions
- A stress ball
- A deck of cards
- Candy
- A zipper lock bag
- Pens
- Paper

There might be other items that come to mind when it
comes to your small group and what works for them. Great!
Add those items to your survival kit and bring them with
you (or leave them in your small group room) just in case
you need a little bit of help.

Remember, if you want this week's small group
conversation to matter more, you want to be ready for
anything.

Prepare for your small group conversation.
PACK A SURVIVAL KIT.

If you want to prepare for your small group
conversation, PRAY for your few.

If you're anything like us, praying for your small group is,
unfortunately, sometimes more of an afterthought than a
vital part of your weekly preparation. Some weeks, you

may only manage a hurried, well-intentioned plea to God on the way to small group. Other weeks, the only time you pray for your few is *during* your small group.

But no matter how many times you've prayed for your few in the last week, month, or year, we've discovered there are at least two reasons why praying for your small group should be an every week kind of thing.

Pray for your few because *they* need it. Being a teenage guy is tough. Besides school, sports, girl drama, breakups, parents, siblings, and everything else your small group is dealing with, every teenage guy is also wrestling with big questions about who they are, why they matter, what they believe and who they'll become. That's a lot for any teenager to manage. So as you prepare for your small group each week, don't forget to pray for your few. They need it.

(And when you pray for your few, don't hesitate to send them a text to let them know you were thinking about them. No matter how old you are, it's always nice to hear somebody's praying for you.)

But there's another reason you should pray for your few.

Pray for your few because *you* need it. When you pray for someone else, it's usually because you want God to do something for them. But what if, when God told us to pray for each other (which He did quite often), He had a second purpose in mind? What if He designed prayer in such a way that praying for someone else didn't just result in change for them? What if it changes *us*, too?

When we pray for someone else, we learn to . . .
consider their needs.
imagine their world.
feel their emotions.
understand their perspective.

One of the most helpful things you can do is pray for a kid (or parent or co-leader) you don't like that much. In other words, **when you pray for the teenagers you lead, you develop more compassion for them.** And as an SGL, you'll need that compassion when . . .
the conversation gets awkward.
when guys relentlessly keep picking on each other.
they ask a tough question.
confidentiality gets broken.

As you prepare for your small group this week, don't let prayer be an afterthought. Be intentional about it. Maybe that means you . . .
pray for a few guys each day.
write their names on your calendar.
set reminders in your phone.

However you decide to remind yourself, make praying for your few a habit. Remember, if you want this week's small group conversation to matter more, you want to have a conversation with God *before* you have a conversation with your few.

**Prepare for your small group conversation.
PRAY FOR YOUR FEW.**

So there you have it. Three ways to **prepare** for your small group conversation every week. We said it would be simple, right?
Read your email.
Rehearse what you'll say.
Pray for your few.

And now that you're (mostly) prepared for your small group conversation, let's talk about how to lead that conversation.

QUIZ:

HOW WELL DO YOU PREPARE FOR YOUR SMALL GROUP?

Throughout this book you'll find a few quizzes we've created as self-evaluation tools. Circle your answers (or just think them), and at the end of this book, you'll be able to see which areas of group conversation you're stellar at as well as the areas where you might have a little room to grow.

Answer honestly, and have fun!

Did you get an email or other communication from your student pastor this week? Did you read it?

Yes   No   Um, I don't know.

Do you pray for your few regularly? You know, *besides the times your few ask tough theological questions?*

Yes   No   Define regularly.

Do you have a system for reminding yourself to pray for your few?

Yes   No   I don't need reminders. I'm
                         amazing.

Do you usually know what your conversation is going to be about *before* you arrive?

Yes   No   Why ruin the surprise?

QUIZ

Do you know the topic so well that you could lead your small group conversation with your eyes closed? Well, we're not saying you should, because that would be weird. But could you navigate most of the conversation with your group *without* looking at your small group questions?

Yes   No   Sometimes

NEXT STEP

We know the art of group talk looks a little different for everyone. Below, write one or two specific and practical things you can do to better **PREPARE** to lead your few this week.

2

chapter
two
connect

Connect

(Talk about something FUN)

Now that you've . . .
read your email
rehearsed what you'll say
packed your survival kit
prayed for your few. . .
you're ready! It's time to finally lead a small
group conversation.

But wait.

What about the guys in your group?
Are *they* ready for your conversation?

Right now, the teenage guys you lead are probably *not*
thinking about your next small group conversation.
More than likely, they're thinking about . . .
their big science test tomorrow,
how they're going to get ungrounded,
who's going to be at practice tonight,
or, if they're in high school, how many hours they have to
work to pay for gas money and concert tickets.

We don't mean to discourage you. It's not that your few
don't care about you, your small group, or their faith. It's
just that they have a lot of other things on their minds.

And that's okay! You don't need your few to come to small
group ready to talk only about forgiveness, prayer, or
the book of Ephesians. You need them to come to small

group ready to talk about *anything*—especially the stuff that matters to them . . . even if that thing is how great the graphics are in the new *Call of Duty*.

In the first few minutes of your small group conversation, your few don't need to immediately dive into that week's discussion questions. **They just need to connect.**

Don't forget that leading a small group is about something much bigger than discussion questions. It's about the relationships you're building over time. But you'll never build a great small group relationship—or have a great small group conversation—if you can't connect first.

How you connect with your small group is simple. For an SGL like you, it may even be obvious. But just so we're all on the same page, let's put it this way:

Before you talk about faith with your small group, you should spend a little time talking about their week.

Before you ask them to be vulnerable, you should probably ask what they're doing this weekend.

And before you tell them to participate, you should make sure they know you're happy to see them.

Here's the point:
Before a teenage guy can ENGAGE in a conversation about a God who cares about him, he may need to CONNECT with people who care about him.

2.1

If you want your small group conversations to matter more,

connect with them

Connect with them

If you're leading a small group of teenage guys, you're probably not a teenager (well, unless you are a teenager). You may have been one at some point, but I'm guessing you're not anymore. And since you're not a teenage guy, it's probably not always going to be easy to connect with the students in your group.

That's because they're not like you. Whether it's the music you listen to, the things you worry about, or the number of emojis you text each day, you and your few are very different people. At least, I hope so. Because they're teenage guys. And you're not.

And they're not like you used to be. You may remember what it was like to be a teenage guy, but things aren't like they were when you were their age. Whether you're in your eighties or your twenties, the world has changed quite a bit since you were a teenager.

So while it may not always be easy to connect with the teenage guys in your small group, if you want your small group conversations to matter more, you've got to start by making a weekly connection with each of your few. If you want your small group to open up, they need to feel connected to you.

Here are three ways to get started . . .

1. CONNECT BEFORE SMALL GROUP

If conversation comes easily for your small group, you probably know what it's like to look at the clock and realize small group ends in five minutes and your group is still answering the question, "How are you?"

And if small talk isn't exactly your small group's favorite hobby, you've probably had weeks when success looked like getting your group to speak in full sentences.

If either of these situations sounds familiar to you, whether you wish your small group time was twice as long or half as short, you might have a connection problem. But don't worry. It has an easy solution.

Connect with your few *before* small group. Some guys have a lot to say to you—more things than could possibly be covered during your small group time. When you connect with those guys before small group, you give them time to share their stories before your small group conversation begins.

Other guys need some time to warm up before they open up to you. When you connect with those guys before small group, you give them time to get comfortable so they're ready to share when your small group conversation begins.

Either way, remember this:

The QUALITY of your small group conversations will reflect the QUANTITY of your connections outside group time.

So, you might want to try . . .
checking in with them during the week.
going to one of their games or activities.
starting a group text conversation.
meeting them at the door.

singing alongside them during worship.
sitting with them during the teaching.
walking with them to small group.

And if you do, you might just find that small talk with a teenage guy is a little different than small talk with an adult. For starters, they're not great at it. Teenage guys have grown up in a world where many of their conversations are typed, not spoken. So if you try making small talk with one of your few and it feels awkward, that's okay. It doesn't mean they don't like you. Like an old television antenna (remember those?), small talk with a teenager can take a few tries and minor adjustments before you get a genuine connection.

Here are a few tricks that have worked for us:

The common ground game. When you chat with a guy, particularly in a new group, ask questions about everything: his favorite movies, what's on his playlist, sports he plays, school clubs, talents, family, everything. Don't let the interaction end until you've said "me too" and found one thing the two of you have in common. Next time you see him, you'll instantly have a conversation starter.

The follow-up. Ask about something he mentioned the last time you saw him. Maybe it was a tough test or a prayer request for his mom. A chat before group is a great time to connect with a guy by following up on what's most important to him. Of course, remembering their hopes, dreams, and prayer requests from week-to-week isn't as easy as it sounds. So, if you need a little help, keep a note on your phone or download the Lead Small app so you can keep track of your few's prayer requests and sneak a peek right before they arrive.

The helpless leader approach. No matter how good your conversation skills are, sometimes it will be painful trying to get any interaction out of one of your few. One way to get them talking is to ask for their help. If you know what they know about, ask them about it! Many guys tend to like talking about shoes, technology, and sports. So try asking something like, "What shoes should I get next?" "What video games are you playing?" or, "Any suggestions for what movie I should go to this weekend?" Be sure to watch for students' unique interests. You'd be amazed what a teenage guy might know about the best domesticated dog breeds, Shakespearean theatre, or rebuilding classic cars.

Making small connections early can make a big impact on your conversation later. That's why one of the best ways to master the art of group talk is to work hard at mastering the art of small talk.

Don't let the first time you connect with your small group be the moment your small group conversation starts. Connect with them and make some small talk *before* small group begins.

2. CONNECT WITH NEW STUDENTS

At some point, chances are someone new will join your small group. And that's a great thing! But let's be honest. It can also be a challenge to add someone new to your group. Will he feel welcome? Will your few like him? Will they have anything in common? And how do you get them to actually talk to one another?

If these are the questions running through your mind, imagine the questions running through his. When you're a teenager, being the new guy can be pretty scary. That's why it's up to you to make him feel welcome, safe, liked, and celebrated.

 SMALL GROUP SURVIVAL KIT: KING SIZE CANDY BAR
Remember that survival kit we told you to pack? Here's the first thing on your list. The

biggest candy bar you can find. When someone new joins your group, it's your job to help them feel connected. Celebrate their first week with your group with the only true way to a teenage guy's heart—food.

In other words, connect with him. Here are a few tips you might want to try . . .

Remember his name. If this doesn't seem like a big deal, it's because you've never seen the look on a teenager's face when he realizes you've forgotten his name.

I (Jeremy) am horrible at remembering names. On many occasions, I've had this experience: I'll meet a new student and he'll tell me his name. I'll enthusiastically welcome him and then roll into the group conversation. After group is done, I'll say something like, "Hey! Thanks for hanging out with us. I really enjoyed having you here and I hope you felt comfortable and got something out of the discussion. Just know we're here for you as a place where you can belong and explore faith. It was so great meeting you, Phil." Then the student will look at me and hesitantly respond with, "Um, thanks, but my name is Bill. Not Phil." Ouch!

Don't let this happen to you! Next time a new student shows up for small group, here's a tip:

1. Say his name out loud.
2. Repeat it.
3. And repeat it again.

Like this: "Your name's Chris? It's so great to meet you. Where do you go to school, Chris?" Repeating his name will help you remember it. And it will let him know you remember it, too.

Learn about him. Most teenage guys will be hesitant to join your small group for the first time. So to help him feel comfortable, learn more about him. Ask about his school, family, and interests. No matter what's going on around you, make him feel like the most important person in the room.

Try something like this:
"Sam, what's one thing you love and one thing you hate about school?"
"Jeremiah, if you could do anything for an entire weekend, what would it be?"

Find common ground. As you learn about who he is, look for ways to connect his experiences with yours.

If he loves music, tell him about your obsession with death metal.
If he plays lacrosse, tell him about your terrible hand-eye coordination.
And if he loves manga but you aren't exactly sure what that is, Google it.

When a new student joins your small group, remember, it's your job to help him feel connected. His experience at church is impacted by his experience with *you*, so don't just connect with the guys you see every week. **Connect with new students, too.**

3. CONNECT DURING SMALL GROUP

No matter how hard you try to connect with each of the guys in your small group before small group begins, there will be weeks when you can't . . .
fist bump every guy.
hear every story.
catch up on every detail.

So as your small group time begins, use the first few moments to connect with the guys you couldn't connect with before small group began.

You might be tempted to dive right into your small group conversation. We get it. You've got a lot to accomplish. But when you take the time to connect with every guy, you're not wasting precious small group time. You're laying a foundation that the rest of your conversation will be built on.

So when small group begins, don't rush your few into the discussion questions. **Connect with them during small group.**

Because if you want this week's small group conversation to matter more, your few need to feel connected to you. **CONNECT WITH THEM.**

2.2

If you want your small group conversations to matter more, help them

connect with each other

Connect with each other

As a small group leader, you're a big deal. You give your few a place to belong. You show them what God is like. You love them, lead them, teach them, and coach them. Without SGLs like you, small groups wouldn't work. Your few need you!

But they also need **each other.**

Because you can't go to school with your few. You're not in third period or the cafeteria or on the bus or at practice with them, but chances are at least some of your few will be in all of those places together. And they will be able to look out for each other, encourage each other and challenge each other in a way that you, as an adult, just can't. **You may have a great conversation on Sunday, but as a group they will face Monday together.**

If you look back at the earliest churches, what you'll see is pretty interesting. You'll see no buildings. No choir rooms. No praise bands. There were no student programs. No Sunday school classes. No fall retreats.

There was simply community. Genuine, pure, tight-knit, nothing-to-hide, kill-my-best-goat-for-you kind of community.

The church wasn't a place. The church was a group.
As an SGL, it's your job to cultivate that kind of community.

To give your few
a tribe.
a safe place.
a small group.

That's why it's not enough for your few to connect with you.
They need to connect with each other, too.

Oh, but—they're teenagers. So they may need a little help
from you.

They need you to connect them with each other.

1. CONNECT THEM WITH AN ICEBREAKER.

You may have spent some time before small group
connecting with each of the guys in your group. But now
that small group has started, this may be the first time this
week they've all connected with one another.

So to help them connect
and to get the conversation started,
ask an icebreaker question.

Icebreaker questions aren't meant to be too deep or
serious—their purpose is to get the conversational juices
flowing. Sometimes, you might choose to ask something
hypothetical, like . . .
- If you could go on a road trip with any celebrity, who
  would you take and where would you go?
- If you could prove the existence of any mythical
  creature, what would you want it to be?
- If you could name the next dinosaur discovered, what
  would you name it?

For some groups, especially in high school, students may be ready to jump into conversation by talking about their weeks. You might start group with a question like . . .

- What were your HIGHS and LOWS from last week?
- What made you MAD, SAD, and GLAD this week?
- What happened since we saw you last?

Something to keep in mind when leading a group of middle schoolers is that they may be nervous to share anything that makes them stand out—after all, in middle school, being different is the worst thing you can be.

That's why middle schoolers will often go with a safe and boring answer, or repeat what everyone else said. So in order to get some original answers, use a totally goofy question like . . .

- Would you rather eat a cottage cheese taco or a yogurt cheeseburger?
- Hot Dog. Sandwich or something else? Explain your view.

Ask an icebreaker question and the group's still quiet?
Call for an all-skate (basically everyone answers).
Or spend some time making up a secret hand-shake for your small group.
Or encourage them to answer the question with the guys sitting directly next to them.

SMALL GROUP SURVIVAL KIT: ICEBREAKER QUESTIONS

Here's the next thing on your packing list. It's not easy to come up with icebreaker questions on the spot. Trust us. We know. We've tried. They're much easier to come up with when you're *not* being stared at by a group of teenage guys (and when you have access to Google). Write down a few of your favorite icebreaker questions, and stash them in your Survival Kit for later. (Or grab a few from us at leadsmall.org!)

A good icebreaker question will give your few a chance to . . .
- talk about themselves (that means no "yes" or "no" questions).
- learn something new about each other (which should be pretty easy once they start talking).
- laugh together (so maybe ask something other than, "What's your favorite Bible verse?).

If they don't laugh together, they'll probably never feel comfortable enough to talk with each other about their questions, their doubts or their life experiences. So help your few connect with each other. **Connect them with an icebreaker.**

2. CONNECT THEM THROUGH THEIR INTERESTS.

Maybe your small group has a lot in common.
Maybe they . . .
have all the same hobbies.
laugh at all the same jokes.
like all the same music.

But probably not.

Most likely, you're probably leading a small group of guys who are all very different. In that case, it's your job to help them discover what they have in common.

Maybe they all love football . . . or Cheetos . . . or fail videos . . . or EDM. If you already know something they all have in common, point out that connection.

As a student pastor, I (Shef) loved watching how some of my best SGLs would do this. They worked hard to figure out things all the kids could connect to. The stranger the better! One of our small group leaders loved bacon, and it turns out every single one of his guys did too! He started a weekly challenge in which the guys had to memorize scripture or do random good deeds. The prize was a box of bacon. You know the pre-cooked, doesn't-need-to-be-refrigerated, how-is-this-even-legal box of bacon? That one. His few went nuts. They began to talk all things bacon. When they went to camp, they wore big, foam bacon hats. We even started to refer to them as the Bacon Bros.

Here's the point, do you think it was hard for this leader to get his guys to talk each week? Nope, they just start talking bacon. So, what is it for you? What could be your group's thing? What is it already? Lean into that and make it work for you. You're group's conversations will be "sizzlin" before you know it. (I apologize . . . I couldn't help myself.)

If you're not sure what your few have in common, turn it into a game. Put five minutes on the clock, and challenge them to find one thing they all have in common.

And if you're pretty sure they have absolutely nothing in common, try watching a video of cats. Cat videos bring everyone together.

So help your few connect with each other. **Connect them through their interests.** (And cat videos.)

3. CONNECT THEM WITH SOMEONE NEW.

It's not always easy for teenage guys to connect with someone new. Even inside your small group, you've probably noticed that some guys don't connect quite as well as others. And that's okay. You can't force your guys to be friends, but you can encourage them to make a new connection.

If you are a high school small group leader you might want to try . . .
splitting into pairs to answer an icebreaker question.
splitting into *new* pairs for the next question.
splitting into even more new pairs until everyone has had a chance to connect with someone new.

But even though splitting into pairs can be a big win in high school groups, it can cause some awkwardness in middle school.
Pair and share is not going to be your friend in middle school.
Groups of three or more are your friend.
Try making teams and playing some sort of game or competition. That way it's not forcing them to have a conversation, but doing something together in order to connect.

Or you could just say . . .
"Hey Wyatt! Did you know Charlie runs track too?"

Whatever this looks like for you, give it a try this week. Help your few connect with each other. **Connect them with someone new.**

And remember, if you want your small group conversations to matter more, you might want to try this before the conversation begins: **Connect with them and help them connect with each other.**

Because before a teenager can connect with God, he may need to connect with *someone* who's connected with God.

QUIZ:

HOW WELL DO YOU CONNECT WITH YOUR FEW?

Group time has started, and it's up to you to get the conversation going in a direction that invites everyone in! Before you can go deeper, it's probably a good idea to connect with your few. Answer the questions below to see how well you **CONNECT** with your few each week.

What's the best way you've found to check in with your few during the week?

Do you show up early enough to connect with each of your guys before small group begins?

QUIZ

Do the guys in your group usually connect with each other before small group begins?

What's your go-to icebreaker question? (You know, other than, "How was your week?")

QUIZ

What was the last thing that made your whole group laugh? Like really hard?

✎

If we picked a random name from your small group roster, could you tell us three things about him?

✎

QUIZ

When a new guy joins or visits your group, how do you help him feel comfortable and connected?

NEXT STEP

We know the art of CONNECTION looks different for everyone. Below, write one or two specific and practical things you can do to better CONNECT with your few before group this week.

3

chapter three
know

Know

(Talk about YOURSELVES)

So let's say you've . . .
prepared for your small group conversation.
connected with your few.
helped your few connect with each other.

Now—*finally*—you can start having a conversation
about faith.

Right?

Well . . .
Almost.
Hang in there for just a few more minutes.

There's one more thing you should probably do before you
have a conversation with your few about faith.

But first, imagine this.

You're at the gym on the treadmill. Another guy gets
on the machine next to you. Everything is normal, when
suddenly he makes eye contact with you and asks,
"So what spiritual battle are you facing right now?" or,
"How are you practicing sexual integrity?" or, "Is there
somewhere in your life you need to repent?"

Um . . . *awkward*, right?

Of course it is! Because we don't have personal,

meaningful, and authentic conversations with people
unless we have a relationship with them that is personal,
meaningful, and authentic.

This is a pretty obvious idea, but one we often need to be
reminded of.

Think about it. Who was the last person you had an
honest
open
meaningful
conversation with?

It probably wasn't a stranger or a random acquaintance.
More than likely, it was your best friend, your mom, your
wife, or your mentor. You know—someone you trust.
Someone who loves you. Someone who knows you.

Teenage guys are no different. They want to have honest
conversations about things that matter—like faith, for
example. But they want to have those conversations with
the right people.

Teenage guys won't have honest conversations with
just anyone.
But they will have them with safe people.
They won't have honest conversations anytime
or anywhere.
But they will have them in safe places.

So if you want to have better small group conversations,
make sure your small group feels like a safe place. And
if you want your small group to feel like a safe place,
make sure your small group conversations don't feel like
conversations with strangers. Make sure your small group is
a place where your few feel known.

But here's the thing about being known.
(It might sound obvious, but stay with us.)

A teenage guy won't feel *known* until someone knows *him.*

If you want the guys in your group to feel known,
you can't force it
and you can't fake it.
The only way to help a teenager feel known
is to **actually know him.**

That's why, as an SGL, it's your job to
know the guys in your group
and to help them know each other.

Knowing—*really knowing*—your small group is a big deal.

**Because before a teenage guy can KNOW *God*
loves him, he may need to be KNOWN by *people*
who know God.**

3.1

If you want your small group conversations to matter more,

know
them

Know them

It's not enough just to **connect** with the guys in your group. You've got to really **know** them—and I don't just mean your favorites. If you want your small group conversations to matter more, you've got to *know every guy*.

So, before you lead a conversation with teenage guys, there are a few things you need to know about teenagers. First, you need to know where your few are at developmentally. You need to understand the phase they're in and all that comes with it emotionally, physically, and socially. *

To get you started, here are some summaries of what guys may be experiencing in each grade (of course, these might not be true of ALL middle and high school guys, but they do apply to MANY of them):

Sixth-grade guys, life is all about figuring out who they like—and who likes them. Your few will likely become obsessed with peer approval, yet be totally unaware of it. They'll go to great lengths to fit in. Friendships change, hormones kick in, and their interests shift. This means creating a safe place in your small group is essential so they have a place they can stop attempting to fit in, and just be themselves.

---

* If you're looking for great resources about the developmental changes students experience from year to year, check out justaphase.com. It's full of resources for parents and leaders just like you—helping you make the most of every phase.

Seventh grade is the year of personal discovery. They'll try things they have never tried before. Not everyone will make the team. Everything about themselves is changing. And everything is done en masse. They walk the hall in pairs. They go to the mall in a herd. They build unfathomably large social media platforms. Planning group outings with your group will be one of the best ways to connect with them, and help them connect with each other.

Eighth graders are beginning to think about who they want to become one day. They realize they don't have to believe what they have been told to believe, and they don't have to behave how they have been told to behave. They'll doubt, question, and debate. They want to make their own decisions. So, help them sort through the options.

Ninth grade is all about finding a group of friends where you fit. Guys may talk a lot about finding or changing friend groups. That means spending extra time connecting is a good idea. And connecting outside group with guys who feel lonely or left out is essential.

Tenth grade is the time when students begin to question everything. Don't panic if your normally agreeable ninth graders are now challenging everything you've taught them. That's normal. Instead, make group conversations a safe place to ask questions and express doubt.

Eleventh grade is when students start driving, working, and dating. That means you may see a drop in small group attendance, but don't let that be where the conversation ends. Stay in touch with those who seem to have checked out, letting them know it's always okay to check back in.

Twelfth-grade guys tend to have equal parts excitement and anxiety about what this last year means for them. This is the time to begin helping them see community is about

the people, not the building or the small group itself.
So spend time with guys outside group, helping them to
connect relationally so they'll still have those friendships
when they leave.

Once you understand some of what's happening
developmentally in the lives of your few, if you want your
small group conversations to matter more, you need to
know every guy personally.

When you know a teenage guy *personally*, you'll know . . .
his name.
his birthday.
his family.
his talents.
his fears.
his hopes.
his food allergies.

When you know him, you'll know about . . .
his week.
his friends.
his exam on Monday.
his game on Friday.
his new crush.
his fight with his dad.
his new shoes that are just "lit."

Maybe that seems like a lot of things to know about every
guy in your group.
We're not saying you need to know
everything that happens
every week
to *every* guy.
Especially if you have 19 guys and counting on your roster.

We're just saying if you want your few to feel known in your
small group, **you're going to need to know them.**

Here are a few ways to KNOW your few . . .

1. KNOW THEIR WORLDS

Remember when we talked about how to PREPARE for your small group conversation? One of the ways we suggested preparing for your conversation was to **consider what's happening in their lives right now.**

It makes sense, right? There are certain things that would be helpful to know before your small group conversation begins.

Before you ask what they're doing this weekend, it would be nice to know Friday is Marko's birthday.

Before you begin a discussion about gossip, you might want to be aware of the rumor Doug started about Josh this week.

Before you lead a conversation about trusting God as a heavenly Father, you should probably know that Sam's dad just left.

If you want to get to know a student's world, it helps to . . .

1. Show up in his world. No matter how much your few tell you about their school, it doesn't compare to seeing it for yourself. If your guys don't drive yet, offer to pick a few of your guys up from practice and show up a little early.

2. Know his family. A middle schooler is beginning to gain his independent identity, but he is still very much a product of his family. The family schedule, plans, friends, and vacations revolve around what the guardian decides. Their plans are made for them most of the time. So walk him out to the car after group to get a minute with his parent, follow his parents on

social media, organize an event that parents can come to, ask the student questions about family traditions, dynamics, and plans in your next one on one. You can tell a lot about a student's world when you know his family, because his family is still so much of his world. Once your few enter high school, it will probably become more difficult to connect with their parents in-person. You might consider sending monthly emails about teaching topics and small group activities that are coming up. Or have a little fun by planning something your few can do together as a group with their parents like a game night, bowling, or paintball.

3.   Engage with his social media. Instagram is like a cheat sheet to see a snippet of your guy's daily life. Or, at least what they want to show the world about their life. When you follow your guys on social media, you get to see the world the way they see it.

4.   Follow who he follows. Most of your few aren't subscribing to magazines or listening to radio stations. The people and bands and companies influencing their worldviews are the ones they follow on social media. So it helps if you follow them too. Do most of your few follow a particular Spotify playlist? Try to listen to it once or twice a week. Do some of them follow a group of celebrities or a TV channel's social media account? Subscribe. We get it. Instagram may not be your cup of tea, but it helps to know what words, images, and ideas feel normal to your few. It gives context to your conversation. So follow who they follow. And if you're not sure, ask them!

One of the clearest examples of this for me (Brett) was that in one of the groups I led, I had multiple boys who did not have either a father or a mother in the picture. Whether it was a result of divorce, incarceration, or the death of a parent, a good chunk of my group never witnessed healthy, loving relationships growing up or had a "normal" relationship with their parents. Because of that knowledge, whenever the series or messages would focus on relationships with parents or dating, there was a lot of adjusting I would need to do in order to include everyone in the conversation.

The more you know about a teenager's world before your small group conversation begins, the better your conversation will be. When you know what's happening in their world, you'll be more likely to know . . .

what **to** say.

what **not** to say.

when to **celebrate** them.

when to **challenge** them.

when to **comfort** them.

SMALL GROUP SURVIVAL KIT: NOISEMAKER

When you know your few, you know when they need to be celebrated. But it's not exactly easy to keep track of everything that's happening in their lives. That's why it's helpful to keep a noisemaker on hand. Try downloading an app that has a sound effect board—specially one with sounds like "crowd goes wild" or "dance party beats." Because whether it's because of a birthday, a report card, a great game, or a new record time in Mario Kart, sometimes one of your few will need to be celebrated—and you'll need to be prepared.

You don't need to know *everything* about your guys' lives before you begin a small group conversation. The truth is that a good small group conversation will probably teach you something new about your few. But you shouldn't have to wait for small group time to catch up on their lives.

So don't.

If you want to know about their worlds . . .
follow them on social media.
text them during the week.
ask how they're doing.
follow up on their prayer requests.
talk with their parents.
If you want your small group conversations to matter more,
it's not enough for you to simply **CONNECT** with your few
each week. You've got to **KNOW** them—*really* know them.
And you can start by **knowing their worlds**.

2. KNOW THEIR PERSONALITIES

This might be a wild guess.
We could be completely wrong.

But we're going to assume that your small group is filled
with a few different types of personalities.

We're also going to assume that managing those
personalities can sometimes be a challenge. Especially
when you're trying to lead a small group conversation.

Some guys dominate the conversation
while others sit quietly.

Some are goofballs
and some are serious.

Some are outgoing
and some are reserved.

Some will follow the group
while some will try to lead it.

Some are self-aware
and some (well, maybe most) are completely oblivious.

It won't always be easy to have a conversation with so
many competing personalities, but here are a few tips that
might help:

Know Your Extroverts They have a lot to say. They like being the center of attention. On a good day, the extroverts in your group probably fill the room with energy, keep the conversation moving, and get everyone laughing. But on a bad day, they leave you with ringing ears, a hoarse voice, and a desperate need for a nap. But no matter what kind of day you have this week with your few, here are a few tips for leading extroverted teenage guys in a small group conversation.

Be patient with them. Remember, your few are not adults—they're teenage guys. They're still learning to be self-aware and emotionally intelligent. In the meantime, if they're too loud, if they interrupt you too often or if they've been talking for longer than you'd like, be patient. When you correct them, correct them with kindness (and maybe even a little humor). Keep in mind that some guys react poorly to being publicly challenged and you may want to talk with them to the side. And remember, if you treat your extroverts with patience, respect, and dignity, they'll be much more likely to use their energy and words for the good of your conversation next time.

Hear them. After they've said what must be their 500,000th word of the day, it's not easy to give your extroverts your full attention. But keep this in mind: If you can give them the focused attention they need for at least a few minutes, they'll be more likely to focus and less likely to continue seeking that attention for the rest of your conversation.

Sit near them. Chances are, they probably know they have a tendency to dominate your small group conversations, but they may need you to help them stay in check. So next week, keep them within arm's reach. If you need to rein them in, try putting a hand on their shoulder as a gentle (and subtle) reminder to do more listening and a little less speaking.

SMALL GROUP SURVIVAL KIT: FOOTBALL
Have you ever led a conversation where everyone had something to say? About *everything*? At the exact same time? In those moments, you need a football (and maybe some ear plugs). Here's how to use it:

Make this rule: "For the rest of small group, you may only speak if you're holding the football." Give the ball to the teenager of your choice. If they follow your instructions, invest $5.00 and buy cupcakes next week as a reward.

Know Your Introverts They're quiet. They're reserved. They sometimes observe your conversations more than they participate (especially if you have a handful of them in your group). Your introverts probably aren't the first to respond to a small group question, but when you can get them to speak, you're usually glad they did. A small group conversation can be an intimidating environment for an introvert, so here are a few tips for keeping them involved in the conversation.

Don't forget them. It's pretty easy to favor your extroverts during a small group conversation. It makes sense. They're always ready to answer even if their answer isn't very well thought out. Introverts may not be as vocal during your small group conversation, but that's not because they're not engaged in it. In fact, they're probably thinking more deeply about your conversation than your extroverts. So in your next small group conversation, don't forget to engage your introverts. They have a lot to contribute.

Don't surprise them. Introverts don't usually like to be put on the spot. There are few things more uncomfortable for an introverted teenage guy than being asked to speak in front of a group unexpectedly. So if you want them to participate, give them a heads up. Say something like, "Hey Kurt, after this, you've got the next question." Or try, "I'd love to hear what you think about this in a second, but let me tell you a story first." You might even want to try slipping them the questions in advance so they can think about their responses before the conversation begins.

Don't force them. As you get to know your introverts, you'll begin to learn when to push them to speak and when to let them sit back and observe. As an SGL, you'll figure out when to challenge your few without making them feel pressured, uncomfortable, or embarrassed.

Keep in mind that your few are also constantly changing during their teenage years. You might see their personalities change a couple times before you move them out to graduate. They're still figuring out who they are and how they want to operate in the world. Be careful not to put them in a box they feel they must live up to. Avoid saying things like:

"That's Karl, he's the funny one of the group," or "Why are you *always* so quiet?"

That doesn't mean you shouldn't do your best to understand their personalities and how they're wired. But remember that their brains will not be fully developed for another 7 to 12 years and you might see some changes in who they are within that time frame.

It's not easy to lead a group filled with competing personalities, but you can do it! The more you get to know your few, the better you'll be at managing the conversation.

If you want to make your small group conversations matter more, you'll need to **KNOW** your few. And you can do that by **knowing their personalities.**

SMALL GROUP SURVIVAL KIT: DECK OF CARDS

Sometimes you need to shift the balance of power between your extroverts and introverts. A great tip we got from a fellow SGL was to always bring a deck of cards to group—regular cards, *Uno* cards, *Candyland* cards—any cards will work. Hand them out at the beginning of your group time, and when it comes to answering questions you can call on all the "blues" or all of the "6s" to answer the next question. Now you've got a reason to let everyone have an equal chance at sharing during group!

3. KNOW THEIR DISTRACTIONS

My (Jeremy) small group of middle school guys meet in a small office in our church. The room is small, cozy, and enclosed. I was positive it would be perfect for an effective, distraction-free small group conversation. And it was!

For five minutes.

Then they discovered the pillows and couch cushions. I guess I thought that they'd experienced sofas at their own homes and wouldn't be able to use anything in this room to be a distraction. But I was wrong. Let's just say our small group conversation was not very effective that first week. The following week, I made an announcement before our small group conversation began: the pillows and cushions were off limits. Problem solved!

At first, they sulked. Then five minutes later, Hoffman had collected all the pillows, sat on top of them, and proceeded to fart on them.

The third week, I had a plan. Before our small group

conversation began, I collected every cushion and pillow in the room. And then I hid them. All of them.

Four months later, the pillows still end up being hidden each week.

Okay, okay. Maybe that wasn't the best approach. Maybe you're thinking I should have . . .
taken charge.
spoken to them about respect.
threatened to call their moms.

And maybe you're right. But you know what?

Sometimes it's just easier to hide the pillows.

Here are just a few examples of distractions that might pop up for middle schoolers:
- Poking each other
- Needing to go to the bathroom
- A squeaky chair
- Hearing other small groups talking or laughing
- Knowing they're going to get donuts after small group
- Or finally, literally *anything*

Common distractions for high schoolers may look more like:
- Girls
- Figuring out the plan for what's happening after group
- A rumor at school
- Texts and notifications
- And finally, girls

One of the things I (Brett) noticed most with high schoolers was their need to connect before we jumped into any deeper conversations. Rarely did I have luck trying to get them to jump off the high dive. When I tried, the group time was filled with distractions as they laughed, told jokes, and tried to send me every message possible that they weren't interested in going where I wanted to lead them. I quickly learned that we had to wade out to the deeper waters together. Sometimes, that meant we spent way more time than I was planning to just connect, catch up, and laugh together. (If you're looking for ideas on how to do this well, bounce back to the section of this book titled Connect.)

 SMALL GROUP SURVIVAL KIT: ZIPPER STORAGE BAG
There are few things more distracting than a phone during a small group conversation with teenage guys. If you've ever had to pause a conversation because someone was texting, posting, direct messaging, talking, or filming, you might want to keep a large zipper storage bag handy. On the weeks you don't want to fight a battle against their phones, start your small group by asking everyone (including you) to drop their phones into the bag until the conversation is over.

Whatever it is for your small group, you might want to pay attention to the things that distract your few from your conversation because when you know what distracts them, you can help eliminate those distractions before they derail your conversation.

If you want to make your small group conversations matter more, you'll need to **KNOW** your few. When you know their worlds, know their personalities and know their distractions, you'll be better equipped to lead your conversations. Because if you want this week's conversation to matter more, your few need to feel known by you. **KNOW THEM.**

3.2

If you want your small group conversations to matter more, help them

know each other

Know each other

You already know how important it is for you to know your few. But just like how you need to help your few connect with each other, you're not the only person your few need to be known by. They need to know, and be known by, each other.

We've already said that before a teenage guy can KNOW *God* loves him, he may need to be KNOWN by *people* who know God. But if you're still not convinced that helping your few get to know each other will significantly impact their faith, then consider this.

Just like the people in ancient times developed their view of God as . . .
the God of Abraham,
the God of Isaac,
or the God of Moses,

you have developed a sense of who God is because you have met . . .
the God of Clark,
the God of Sam,
or the God of Jeff.

Here's the point. God has always used people to demonstrate His story of redemption.

It was true then. And it's true today.

It was true for you. And it's true for your few.

So if you want a teenage guy to know God, maybe one of the most important things you can do is to give him a community of people who will talk with him, hang out with him, and do life with him. People who know God and who know him.

You're one of those people.
But you're not the only person he needs.
He needs to know (and be known by) you.
But he needs to know (and be known by) the rest of his small group too.

So make sure you know your few. Then help them know each other.

Here are a few ways to do that . . .

1. MAKE GROUP MEMORIES

Nothing creates a connection like a shared memory.

If you want to move your few
from casually **connecting** with each other
to really **knowing** each other,
you might want to consider making some
memories together.

When you make memories together *outside* of small group, instead of only seeing each other *inside* of small group, you'll help your few know each other better. And when they know one another better, they'll have better conversations.

Cook a meal together.
Go hiking.
Ride a roller coaster.
Build something.
Camp out.

Go on a road trip.
Cheer one of them on in their big game.
Make up a new sport.
Try that impossible trick shot until someone makes it, then
scream until your throats are sore.

When you're back together *inside* of small group, take
time to talk about the memories you made *outside* of small
group. And then make plans to make some new ones. It'll
help your few know each other. And, it will help them grow
together. When you're building new relationships, shared
memories are like the cement. You'll need lots of them,
but it'll make your foundation strong. So **make group
memories** together.

2. BUILD GROUP IDENTITY

We are all created for community.
We all want a place to belong.
We all long to be part of . . .
A group.
A family.
A tribe.

We all want to know these people are our people.

If you don't believe me, go to a football game sometime.
Check out the team colors. The face paint. The screaming.
Now *those* people are passionate about their tribes.

Your few are no different. Okay, they probably don't paint
their faces and scream during small group (or maybe they
do), but it's still true. No matter how cool for school some
of them might act at times, the guys in your small group
want a place to belong. They want a tribe, a family, and a
group that they can call their own.

If you want your small group to really know each other, you

might want to help them see themselves as a group by building a stronger group identity.

How? Well, you could try . . .
starting a group text.
planning a small group hangout.
making matching T-shirts.
sitting together during the service.
inventing a new small group tradition.
having an inside joke.

I (Shef) discovered this accidentally. Each year, our church takes sixth graders to what we call Boot Camp. We split small groups into companies and each company gets a different colored T-shirt. One time, a guys small group assigned to Papa Company weren't thrilled when they saw their purple shirts. But then, for whatever reason, they decided to embrace it. From that day forward, their entire group would wear purple every Sunday and to every event. To them, purple was no longer a color they weren't sure about—it was part of their group's DNA.

When your few have a strong sense of group identity, they'll feel like a tribe, a family and a group. They'll feel like they belong. And when they feel like they belong, they'll be more likely to open up. So help your few know each other. **Build group identity** together.

3. SET GROUP GUIDELINES

If you want your few to know each other, making memories and building group identity will help. But if you want your few to really know each other, they need to feel safe enough to be . . .
real.
vulnerable.
honest.

That's where confidentiality comes in.

But since you're a small group leader, you probably know that confidentiality isn't exactly easy to monitor. You typically won't know about a breach until after . . .

Joel told that girl that Billy has a crush on her.
Francis ratted out Bobby for the periodic table cheat sheet he made.
Parker posted that embarrassing picture of Ben from camp.

We would all *love* to have the perfect group filled with enough respect and maturity to know for sure that what is said in group stays in group. In fact, that should probably be a rule you set up in the beginning. Absolute, 100 percent, swear-on-my-brand-new-iPhone confidentiality should always be your goal. But as the grown-ups, we have to be realistic.

You probably won't be able to prevent every breach in confidentiality, but you can challenge your few to set guidelines that will help your small group feel safe.

And since they're teenagers, it's probably a good idea to let them be part of the guideline setting process. When they're part of the process of setting group guidelines, they'll be more likely to feel responsible for maintaining them.

So **set some group guidelines.** Together.
You might want to start by asking them . . .
What will our group always do?
What will our group never do?
How will we treat each other?

The thing with high school guys is that they'll answer these questions with exactly what you're looking for. You don't have to sell them on the idea of having group guidelines. The challenge is selling them on actually doing it.

We have found it helpful not only to remind guys what our group guidelines are, but why we have them in the first place. The conversation might go something like this:

You: So what happens if someone breaks confidentiality in our group?
Guys: We kill them!
You: Um, no. Seriously. What would *really* happen?
Guys: No one shares anymore.
You: Sort of. People will probably still talk since 30 minutes of silence is weird.
Guys: No one would share anything real. We'd all just give easy answers and be . . . well, fake.
You: Exactly. So the real question isn't "Will we protect confidentiality?" The real question is "Do we want to come to a group every week where people are real or where people are fake?"

This reveals that when you set group guidelines, your few will be much more likely to feel safe enough to be honest in your small group conversations. And honesty is a crucial part of getting to know each other. Help your few know each other. **Set group guidelines** together and remind your few of them often.

Note on confidentiality: As a small group leader, your few might open up to you about some serious stuff. If one of your few shares something that qualifies as one of the three hurts— hurting themselves, hurting others, or being hurt by another—you should talk to your church staff.

If you want your small group conversations to matter more, you might want to make this part of your weekly conversation: **know them and help them know each other.**

Because before a teenager can know *God*, he may need to be known by *someone* who knows God.

QUIZ:

HOW WELL DO YOU KNOW YOUR FEW?

Red Bull or Gatorade? Sports team or band mate? Chipotle or Taco Bell? Xbox or Playstation? Answer the questions below to see how well you **KNOW** your few.

How well do your few know each other? Do they know each other's . . . (circle yes or no)

Names?	yes	no
Birthdays?	yes	no
Favorite sports team?	yes	no
Pet peeves?	yes	no

Which of your few do you know the least? (Write his name here and set a reminder in your phone to connect with him outside group some time this week.)

QUIZ

List two or three of your favorite small group memories.

✏️

How comfortable are your few with being open and honest during your small group conversations?
(circle one)

Not At All   Too Comfortable

NEXT STEP

Getting to know your group looks a little different for everyone. Below, write one or two specific and practical things you can do to get to **KNOW** your few even better this week.

✏️

4

chapter four
engage

Engage

(Talk about the TRUTH)

Okay.
Finally.
This is the part you've been waiting for.

Now that you've'
prepared for your small group conversation,
connected as a group,
and gotten to **know** each other,
you're ready to actually **engage** your small group in
a conversation.

But not just any conversation.
A really important conversation.
A conversation about authentic faith.

After all, that's why you became an SGL in the first place,
isn't it? So you could lead teenagers in conversations about
truths that will shape their faith and future.

Sure, it's taken us some time to get here, but that was
intentional. Before we could talk about building authentic
faith in your small group, we had to talk about building
authentic relationships first.

When you take the time to invest relationally in your
few by . . .
connecting with them
helping them connect with each other
knowing them
helping them know each other

. . . you lay a foundation of trust, influence and relationships that you're going to need if you want your few to ultimately engage in a conversation about faith. But before we go any further, let's clarify something.

Let's talk about that word **ENGAGE.**

Maybe we could have called this chapter **TALK.**
Or **DISCUSS.**
Or **PARTICIPATE.**
Although talking, discussing, and participating are some of the things you probably hope your small group will do, those words don't quite capture the goal of a small group conversation. Not completely.

You see, when you're finally ready to begin a conversation about authentic faith with your small group, your goal isn't for them to simply talk, discuss, or *participate* in your conversation.

When your few participate in a conversation, they might . . .
listen.
respond.
be respectful.
summarize.

But when they *engage* in a conversation, they'll do more than participate. They will . . .
think.
share.
question.
discuss.
debate.
own.
personalize.

But with teenage guys, engagement can be tricky—at least, when you're talking about faith. If you're discussing sports or movies, engaging teenage guys in a conversation is simple. But when you're not talking about Netflix or food—when you're talking about doubt or forgiveness or prayer or sexual integrity—how do you move your few beyond simply *participating* in the conversation?

How do you **ENGAGE** them in a conversation about authentic faith?

Learning to engage your few in your conversations won't always be easy. You won't always get it right. It won't always come naturally. But no matter how your small group conversation went *last* week, there is always something you can do to better engage your few *next* week.

So if you want to better engage your few in your small group conversations, there are a few things you'll probably need to do *less*. You may need to . . .
talk less.
control less.
script less.

And there are a few things you'll probably need to do *more*. Like . . .
listen more.
lead more.
improvise more.

As you work to better engage your few in conversations about faith, there will still be weeks when you'll feel frustrated. There will still be weeks when you'll wish you'd said or done or handled things differently. There will still be weeks you'll wonder if you're really cut out for this small-group-leading thing.

We know. We've been there.

Leading a small group can be difficult. And trying to engage a group of teenage guys in a conversation about authentic faith might be the most difficult part.

So on the weeks when it's difficult to engage your few in a faith conversation, it wouldn't hurt to remember this.

Your few won't remember every small group conversation you'll ever have. But they will remember more than you think.

Even on the weeks when you're sure they weren't engaged in your conversation, **what gets said in small group probably has more of an impact than you think it does.** The words your few share in small group may seem like small things, but they have tremendous influence.

Remember what we said earlier? **Your small group conversations matter**—maybe more than you think. But with the right amount of preparation, relationships, technique, and patience, you can **make your small group conversations matter even more.**

So if you want to make your small group conversations matter more (and we know you do), then you might want to be more intentional about how you engage your few during your conversations about faith.

Because before a teenage guy can ENGAGE in a life of authentic faith, he may need you to ENGAGE him in a conversation about authentic faith.

And here are three ways to do just that.

4.1

If you want your small group conversations to matter more,

speak less, listen more.

(Let's talk about you.)

speak less, listen more

We may not know you, but if you're leading a small group of teenage guys, we're going to guess you took this job because . . .
you love God.
you love teenagers.
you want to tell teenagers about God.

But trying to tell teenagers everything you know about God probably isn't the most effective way to influence their faith. If simply *telling* teenagers what to believe led to a more authentic faith, we wouldn't even need small groups. We could just preach longer sermons.

You know better, though.
You know the power of a small group.
You know the importance of a community.
And you know the impact you can have on a teenager's faith through conversation.

Teachers know this too. That's why they assign group projects, give lab partners, have class discussions, and encourage classroom debates. Teachers understand that teenagers learn better in environments that are collaborative and conversational than they do in lectures. Maybe that's because of how teenagers' brains are developing during this phase.

Or because they're learning to understand multiple points of view.
Or because they tend to trust their peers more than they trust adults.
Or because they're occasionally skeptical of authority figures.
Or because they often process ideas better when they talk about them out loud.
Or maybe it's because of all these things.

In fact, as former teacher (Shef), I experienced the value of engagement all the time. When I asked students to simply recall or summarize what they learned, they would soon forget it. But when I crafted lessons around debating, discussing, and personalizing—in other words engaging—with each other, the students were always more likely to remember it down the road. And even though your role as an SGL isn't supposed to look like that of a classroom teacher, engaging your few in a conversation will go a long way in making the conversation stick. And that's what we want, right?

Whatever the reasons, it's true. Whether the topic is algebra, chemistry, or the Great Commandment, teenagers learn best when they can . . .
talk about it.
ask questions.
share their opinions.
find answers together.
teach someone else.

But sometimes SGLs forget about that.
Sometimes we want to be the person who . . .
talks about it.
asks the questions.
shares our opinions.
has all the answers.

If you want your small group conversations to matter, you have to let them be conversations and not just lessons. Because, you see, you're not a teacher. You're a small group leader. And as an SGL, you'll need to talk sometimes. But more importantly, you'll need to listen.

In fact, we recommend sticking with The 80/20 Rule. In every small group conversation, you should spend at least 80 percent of your time listening, and only 20 percent of your time talking.

That's what we mean by speaking less and listening more.

Okay, we know. The 80/20 Rule might seem unrealistic. Depending on the particular group of teenagers you lead, maybe it is. If that's the case, make it The 70/30 rule! The principle is still the same: **speak less, and listen more.**

But here's the thing. Even when we try to be better listeners, we're usually not very good at it. In fact, when one of your few is speaking, you will probably only pay attention to 48 percent of what he says. And of the 48 percent that you hear, you'll only remember 50 percent of it. (These numbers are entirely made up, but we're pretty sure they're accurate.) But don't feel too bad about it. It's not just you. We're all far worse at listening than we probably think we are.

But if you want to engage your few in a better small group conversation, you'll need to become a better conversationalist. And that starts with being a good listener. Being a good listener takes practice. So here are four steps you can take to **speak less and listen more.**

1. LOOK

Now, this might sound obvious, but stick with us. When one of the guys in your small group is speaking, **look at him.**

(I told you it might sound obvious.)

But if we're honest, we'd probably all agree that making eye contact during a conversation isn't always easy or natural.
Especially when there are so many interesting things happening on your phone.
Or when you can't remember which question you're supposed to ask next.
Or when the guys to your left are discussing their plans for the weekend in what they probably think are whispers, but are definitely not whispers.

Making eye contact with your few isn't always easy (especially in a small group setting), but it's a big deal.

When you look at your few as they speak, you communicate that what they say matters. And if they believe what they say matters, they'll be a lot more likely to keep talking. So put the phone down and **look when they're speaking.**

2. FOCUS

Looking at your few when they're talking is a great step toward becoming a better listener, but it's only the first step. If a guy in your group is talking and you're busy . . .

rehearsing what you'll say next
wondering if your voice cracked that much when you were his age
thinking about your plans after group

. . . then it doesn't matter how well you've maintained eye contact. Your listening skills still need some work.

We have a friend named Heather. Heather is a middle school pastor in Minnesota, and she's one of the best listeners we know. That's why when Heather told us she had a trick for becoming a better listener, we knew we had to . . . well, listen. Heather said that when a student is speaking, asking a question, or telling a story, she imagines she's wearing a set of blinders. (When Heather told us this, she actually put her hands on either side of her face, just in case we didn't get the picture.) She told us that those imaginary blinders are a reminder to stay focused on the student in front of her no matter what. If someone tries to interrupt, or her phone vibrates or she gets hit in the back of the head with a dodgeball, Heather is committed to staying focused on the student in front of her.

The second step to becoming a better listener is to **focus on what he's saying.**

3. SUMMARIZE

Once you've mastered the art of looking and focusing while one of the guys in your group is speaking, it's time to take your listening skills one step further. Once you've heard what he's said, take a second to **summarize what you heard.**

We've already said that we're not always the best listeners. But teenage guys aren't exactly the best communicators either. They can be . . .
long-winded.
hasty.
sarcastic.
off-track.

(Okay, let's face it—so can we.)

Your teenage guys might even tell stories so long that, when they end, no one can remember why they were being told in the first place. That's why summarizing is so important. When you summarize what your few have said, you help the conversation move forward.

You might say something like . . .
"So to summarize, _____ ."
"In other words, _____ ."
"So you're saying, _____ ."
"You're telling me _____ ."

When you summarize what you've heard, you . . .
let them know you're listening.
make sure you understand.
help clarify their thoughts for the rest of the group.
lead the conversation.

The third step to becoming a better listener is
to **summarize.**

4. ASK

After you've summarized what one of your few has said,
don't move on until you've **asked** him this question: "Did I
get that right?" Because the reality is no matter how great
you are at listening to a teenage guy, you will sometimes
misunderstand what he's trying to say.

So when you've summarized what he said, ask if you
understood him. There are two ways he could respond.

1. He could correct you. If he does, that's great! It means
you're getting clarity.
2. He could agree with you. Your guy now feels heard,
known, understood and he is probably more likely to
engage in conversation in the future. But just a word
of caution: It could also mean he feels uncomfortable
correcting you. That's why knowing your few is so
important. The more you know them, the more likely you'll
be able to discern when they're being open and when
they're holding back.

So before you move on to the next question, **ask if you
understood him.**

If you want to make your small group conversations matter more, you'll need to **ENGAGE** your few in those conversations. And this starts with becoming a better listener. So when your few open up, don't forget to look, focus, summarize and ask. That's what it means to **speak less and listen more.**

QUIZ:

HOW WELL DO YOU LISTEN TO YOUR FEW?

Here's a few questions you should ask yourself to see if you're a good listener.

When someone in your group is talking, how often do you try to finish his sentences? (circle one)

Not often   All the time   Only with the eternal talker

When you're telling a story, what are some signs that your few have definitely stopped listening? (draw or write them here)

....

....

....

....

....

....

....

....

QUIZ

When one of your few is telling a story, what are some things that make it difficult to stay focused?

🖉

What percent of your small group conversation do you usually spend speaking? (Pick an actual number)

🖉

NEXT STEP

We know the art of **LISTENING** looks different for everyone. Below, write one or two specific and practical things you can do to better **LISTEN** to your few this week (even the one whose story from last week made you pray for the fire alarm to go off).

4.2

If you want your small group conversations to matter more,

control less, lead more.

(Let's talk about your questions.)

control less, lead more

When you're preparing to lead a small group conversation, it's a good idea to **think with the end in mind.** Thinking with the end in mind means deciding where you want your small group conversation to go. When you identify a destination before your conversation begins, you'll be a lot more likely to actually get there.

After all, you're the small group leader. So if you're going to lead a conversation with your few, you should have an idea of where you're leading them.

So what's your destination exactly? Well, this changes every week.

If your student pastor sends you a weekly update through email or an app, your destination might already be determined for you. To find out, open your weekly communication (if you've got one), and look for a summary of that week's conversation. If you're really lucky, your student pastor may have even summarized the topic into a catchy bottom line like . . .
Remember God is with you.
Make the wise choice.
Be the friend you want to have.

That summary, or bottom line, is your student pastor's destination. It's what they'll be teaching. It's the one idea they hope the teenagers in your ministry will learn and remember all week long.

But that's not *your* destination.
Well . . . okay, it's *almost* your destination.
But not exactly.

You see, if you were **teaching** teenagers, your destination would be to help them **learn** or **remember** what you've taught.

But you're not a teacher. You're a small group leader. So your destination isn't just to help them learn or remember what they've heard from your student pastor. Your destination is to help your few **personalize** and **apply** what they've heard.

Let's say your student pastor is teaching, "Make the wise choice." Then your destination for your small group conversation might be to help each of your students identify one thing they can do to start making wiser choices.

If your student pastor is teaching, "Remember God is with you," your destination might be to challenge your few to consider how their lives might be different if they really believed God was with them.

See the difference?

In large group, the destination is **knowledge.**
In small group, the destination is **application.**

So you've got your destination in mind. Great.
Now you just have to get your group from where they are to where you want them to go.

Easy, right?

(If you answered yes, we're not convinced you've ever met a teenage guy before. The only place it's easy to get a teenage guy to go is out for pizza.)

So how do you get your few to your destination? We're so glad you asked!

You have two options.
You can control them (or at least try).
Or you can lead them somewhere.

Some SGLs make the mistake of trying to control their small group conversations. They know where they're going. They know how to get there. They have a map. They have a schedule. They're going to make sure their few get to their destination no matter what. And they're definitely not going to sightsee or stop for Doritos® on the way.

That approach is probably helpful if you're trying to get to a flight on time, but it's not the best way to approach your small group conversations.

When you try to **control** your small group conversation . . .
it's difficult to adjust or improvise.
your way becomes the right way.
your questions usually have right answers.
you don't view disagreement as an option.
your few may follow you . . . but not willingly.

But there's a second way to approach your small group conversations.

SGLs who have learned how to lead—rather than control—a small group conversation still know where they're headed and how to get there. But they're comfortable with detours, Dorito® stops, and taking the scenic route. They know not everyone will arrive at their destination at the same time, and they understand that they'll need to change their destination completely on occasion. But no matter where they're headed, they're committed to leading their few toward their destination—even if it takes a little longer to get there than they had originally planned.

When you **lead** your few in a small group conversation . . .
you can manage rabbit trails.
you admit you don't have all the answers.
your questions are open-ended.
you encourage discussion and debate.
you value their opinions and ideas.
your few follow you willingly.

As an SGL, we understand the temptation to want to push your few toward the destination in every conversation. With so much at stake, it makes sense. But here's the bad news. You can't actually control your few. So when you make room for side-tracks, debates and left turns, you recognize that, while you can't control your few, you can still lead them.

But maybe all this talk about detours and Doritos® has made you a little uneasy (or hungry). Maybe you're wondering how, exactly, to go about leading a small group conversation without controlling it.

We're so glad you asked.

It's not always easy to give up control. But if you want to engage your few in a better small group conversation, you'll need to become a better leader—not a controller—of your small group conversations. And that starts with the kinds of questions you ask. So here are three things you can do to **control less and lead more.**

1. ASK BETTER QUESTIONS

In case no one has told you this already, let us be the ones to break it to you.

As an SGL, your job is not to be an answer giver.
Your job is to be a question asker.

That's a relief, right? You don't actually have to give correct answers to every question a teenage guy asks as though you're a walking, talking Biblical encyclopedia. If the job of a small group leader was to have all the right answers, your volunteer application process probably should have been a lot more difficult.

If it hasn't happened already, one of your few will eventually ask you a difficult question. If you don't have a perfect answer, it's okay to say, "I don't know."

But since your job is to be a question asker, here's an even better idea. Even if you do have the perfect answer to that tricky question, don't always give an answer. Instead, ask more questions.

As an SGL, questions are your most important tool. A good question can help you . . .
learn about your few.
understand their perspectives.
make them think.
take them on a journey.

And a good question will help the guys in your small group . . .
clarify their beliefs.
reconsider their perspectives.
change their opinions.
identify a next step.

So since the questions you ask are such an important tool, let's talk about how to ask the right ones—questions that don't control your few but lead them somewhere.

Questions that control are questions whose answers are often . . .

one word.
fact-based.
yes or no.
right or wrong.

These are questions like . . .
Did you like the talk this week?
Is gossip a sin?
Who was the apostle Paul?
Don't you agree that _____ ?

But then there are better questions—questions that
lead your few toward your destination but don't control
their journey.

These questions don't ask for answers. They invite
responses. These questions . . .
are open ended.
are opinion based.
invite feedback.
don't have a right answer.

These are questions like . . .
What would it look like if you _____ ?
What do you think about _____?
What do you think would happen if _____?
What's one thing you can do this week to _____?

In a small group conversation, the best kinds of questions
are questions that ask your few to share their experiences,
their opinions, their observations, and their ideas. They're
questions that expect disagreement and encourage
discussion. And they're questions that invite your few to
think, debate, and come to conclusions together. That's
what it looks like for your few to engage in a conversation
instead of just participate. If those aren't the kind of
questions that came in your email, that's okay! You read it
ahead of time and you're able to make some changes.

So if you want to better engage your few by controlling less and leading more, **start by asking better questions.**

2. VALUE SILENCE

This may be difficult to believe, but it's true. Silence in a small group conversation can actually be your friend. Seriously! Sometimes a little silence is exactly what you need.

Okay, we know. Silence in a small group can be awkward. If you ask a question and no one responds within three seconds, you might sometimes go into a mental tailspin. *Was that a stupid question?*
Did it even make sense?
Why aren't they talking?
They're never going to talk.
This is a disaster.
Do they all hate me?

Sure, sometimes your group will be silent because you asked a dumb question. But most of the time, your question was probably just fine.

Don't rush to fill the silence with an answer or a quick change of subject. If you can get comfortable with silence, you can use it. Let them . . .
sit.
think.
process.

And while you wait . . .
gather your thoughts.
watch their body language.
check the clock.
breathe.

When silence sets in, time moves slowly. Ten seconds might feel like five minutes—especially if you're uncomfortable.

Chances are, your few are just as uncomfortable with the silence as you are. If you can be patient, someone will break the silence. So after you ask the question, give them fifteen seconds to respond. If no one has spoken up after fifteen seconds, then you might want to think about rephrasing your question. But before you dive in to rescue them from the silence, give it time.

I (Brett) had a professor in college that, at the time, I did not enjoy. It wasn't because he was a bad teacher, or mean, or boring. It was because he loved silence. Where most teachers would ask a question and re-explain or move on to something else, this professor would just sit in the silence. He knew that, in the silence, one of two things were likely to happen. One, we might get uncomfortable enough in the silence to learn to speak up and dialogue with one other. Or two, we would take a moment to process the information.

Too often, we take silence as an indicator that we're not leading well. In reality, silence in our group is merely breeding ground for what we want to happen.

We have an SGL friend who's so intentional about this. Each week she brings a water bottle, and each time she asks a question, she takes a drink while waiting on her group to respond. Try this with your group! If one guy responds, take another drink while waiting on another. The few seconds it takes to chug some water are hopefully enough to keep you from answering the question yourself (and it'll keep you hydrated).

Try to challenge yourself to wait after asking a question before you speak. If you pay attention, you might even learn something during those 30 seconds of unspeakable torture. Do they look like they're thinking? That's a good thing! Do they look confused? You may need to reword your question. Are they all avoiding eye contact? The question may be too personal. Are they smirking or glancing nervously at each other? You may have uncovered a topic they talk about outside of small group but are embarrassed to talk about inside of small group.

Leading a small group conversation isn't easy when you feel like you're getting the silent treatment. But if you want to better engage your few in conversation by controlling less and leading more, learn to **value silence.**

3. UNDERREACT

Sometimes it's the silence of your few that causes you stress. Other times, one of your few will say something so shocking that you'd happily trade it for an entire day of awkward silence.

Because, you see, controlling less and leading more can be risky.

When you . . .
ask questions that are open-ended,
welcome their opinions and feedback,
encourage discussion and debate,
. . . you won't always be able to anticipate what they'll say.

And if your small group is a place where your few feel safe enough to be honest, your questions might actually prompt someone to be honest.

Honest about what he thinks.
Honest about what he believes.
Honest about what he's done.

When one of your few says something in group that surprises you, you might feel like you've lost control.

You haven't.

Take a breath.
Freak out on the inside.

Thank him for sharing.
And ask more questions.

But when one of your few shares something shocking,
there's one question you should be very careful (and avoid)
asking: *Why?*
Why do you think that?
Why don't you believe that?
Why did you do that?

Asking *why* might feel like a reflex. It will be on the tip of
your tongue. When a teenager confesses something that
shocks you, *why* will seem like the right thing to ask.

When you ask *why*—especially immediately after a
teenager has opened up to you—you will lose your
opportunity to have a conversation. And without a
conversation, you will lose your opportunity to lead him
somewhere new.

That's because the question *why* shuts down a
conversation. It makes them feel stupid or judged or
ashamed. The same is true for adults. Chances are if we do
something wrong, we know it's wrong. So, when we hear
why, we feel like we're being judged. We want to defend
ourselves. We want to put up walls.

That doesn't mean you shouldn't ask any questions. It
just means you should ask different questions—maybe
questions that don't start with *why*. Like . . .

How do you feel about what happened?
What led you to this decision?
What kind of impact do you think this will have on your life,
your relationships, or your faith?
What advice would you give someone else in the
same situation?

When you decide not to ask *why*, even when you're
freaking out on the inside, you invite a conversation,
instead of shutting it down.

When you avoid asking *why*, you . . .
show curiosity instead of judgment.
seek to understand instead of being understood.
choose to listen instead of panic.

Remember, communication goes beyond the words we
say. Watch your eyes, tone, and posture to be sure they're
actually hearing what you are trying to communicate.

When you underreact instead of overreact, you prove
to your few that your small group really is a safe place.
And you can also model for your few what grace and
compassion look like so they will know how to respond
when a friend tells them something shocking. Because
if you want your few to engage in your small group
conversation, you'll need to help them see your group is
a safe place to talk about anything—even the things that
shock you.

So if you want your small group conversations to matter
more, ask better questions, value silence, and underreact.
And remember that you're not the small group controller.
You're the small group leader. So **control less, and
lead more.**

QUIZ:

HOW WELL DO YOU LEAD YOUR FEW?

This is what makes an SGL different than a Sunday school teacher—you've got to be a master conversationalist. And you've chosen to be a leader. So, you've got to keep learning to master the art of group talk. Here are a few quick questions to see how well you lead your group.

When was the last time your group felt out of control? What happened?

Have you ever held your group hostage while you
discussed every single question on your small group guide?

What's the best conversation your few have had in group
recently? What sparked the conversation?

When was the last time your small group went silent?
How did you handle it?

Next time one of your few shares something shocking,
what's one thing you can do to be sure you underreact
(besides practicing your best poker face in the mirror)?

NEXT STEP

We know the art of LEADING looks different for everyone. Below, write one or two specific and practical things you can do to better LEAD a conversation with your few this week.

4.3

If you want your small group conversations to matter more,

script less, improvise more.

(Let's talk about your plan.)

script less, improvise more

As you prepare for your small group conversation each week, you probably have an idea in mind of how the conversation will go. That's great! Having a plan is an important part of preparing for your small group conversation. But as you prepare, rehearse, and read your small group questions in advance, keep in mind:

There's no script for a small group conversation.
At some point, things will not go according to plan.
And you will probably have to improvise.

There's a principle in improv comedy called the "Yes, and . . . " principle. The idea is the comedian will see whatever situation, no matter how absurd, no matter how impossible and say yes. They won't quit. They won't try to force the situation to be more rational. They simply jump in and roll with it. They say yes (either verbally or inwardly) and then build on whatever is already happening.

It starts by saying "Yes." When you say yes, you agree to accept whatever situation, story, or energy the rest of your group throws your way.

"Yes, I am dressed like a hot dog."

"Yes, we are on the moon."
"Yes, I am a little grumpy today."

And when you take your "Yes" a step further by saying, "Yes, and . . . " you not only accept what's been thrown at you, but you also build on it.

Like this . . .
"Yes, I am dressed like a hot dog, and I'm also late for my doctor's appointment."
"Yes, we are on the moon, and hey—it's made of ice cream!"
"Yes, I am a little grumpy, but that's because my eyebrows are missing."

You probably will never lead a small group while on the moon or dressed like a hot dog. (But I've seen the kinds of games student pastors play, so maybe that whole missing your eyebrows situation is not all that unrealistic.) But here's the point. If you want to engage your few in better conversations, you're going to need to be ready to improvise—to take whatever your few throw at you, and then build on it.

Most of the time, you'll only need to improvise a little.
Like when a question isn't working.
Or your few are too fidgety.
Or too talkative.
Or you have a first-time visitor.

But other times, you may need to throw away your plan entirely.
Like when 20 guys show up.
Or only one guy shows up.
Or one of your few experiences a tragedy.

As SGLs who have been forced to improvise more times than we can count, we want to tell you something we wish someone had told us.

You're *allowed* to improvise.
In fact, you should probably *plan* on it.

Because if you want to engage your few in a better small group conversation, you'll need to get comfortable with being uncomfortable. And that starts by letting go of your plan, saying "Yes, and . . . " and choosing to **script less, and improvise more.**

Here are four ways to do that.

1. CHANGE THE QUESTION

You won't always be able to predict the kinds of questions that will work for your small group. Sometimes a question may take you by surprise and start a great conversation. Other times, what you thought was a great conversation starter may result in blank stares and looks of utter confusion.

Sometimes your few might have trouble responding to one of your open-ended questions. That could be because the question is confusing, or maybe it's just because they're a little tired that day. But if your few are having trouble answering an open-ended question, go ahead—change the question.

Here's an example.

Let's say your few are struggling to respond to the question, "How close do you feel to God right now?" Maybe the question was a little *too* open ended. Maybe they're not sure how to put their responses into words. If they're having difficulty, ask the question again. But this time, give them a few options to choose from like: "On a scale of 1–5, how close do you feel to God right now?"

In a small group conversation, open-ended questions are usually best. But when your few are struggling to respond, turning an open-ended question into a multiple-choice question can help narrow their options.

Or maybe the problem isn't the question. Maybe your few aren't responding because their responses would be too personal, or intimate, or embarrassing. If that's the case, you don't need to throw away the question entirely. You just need to make it a little less personal.

So instead of asking them when was the last time they lied, you might say, "Tell me about a time someone lied to you." Or instead of asking which sin tempts them the most, you could ask, "What's one thing people your age are often tempted by?" Teenagers aren't always good at talking about themselves, but they're usually great at talking about other people.

In a small group conversation, it's good to ask tough questions. But when a question seems a little *too* tough for your few, making the question feel a little less personal can get the conversation moving again.

No matter how much you plan for your small group, your conversation can't be scripted. That's why it's so important to improvise. So if you want to better engage your few by **scripting less and improvising more, change a question or two.** You have permission!

2. TRY AN ACTIVITY

Sometimes changing a question is all the improvisation you'll need to help your conversation get unstuck. But other times, you may need to try something a little more drastic. Okay, maybe drastic isn't the right word. We don't mean to scare you.

But on the weeks when your group is too talkative, not talkative enough, goofy, restless, or distracted, you might want to move away from your typical conversation and try something more hands on.

Maybe you've already improvised by changing an open-ended question into a scale question, like, "On a scale of 1–5, how close do you feel to God right now?" To turn that scale question into an activity, you might try this: "On a scale of *this* wall to *that* wall, stand in the place that represents how close you feel to God right now."

Or you could hand out pens and paper. Then ask your few to write down their responses to a question or two. When they're finished writing, you could . . .
read their responses out loud.
ask them to read their own responses out loud.
post them on a wall or bulletin board.

Or you can make a small group video about what you've been learning. Ask each of your few to share what they're learning in 30 seconds or less. Then use your phone to edit their clips into a complete video.

Or you might decide to break up the group dynamics by splitting into pairs. When everyone has a partner, spend time praying together or discussing questions one at a time.

Or maybe you ask your few to work together on a project, challenge, or action step together. Give them something tangible to do that helps them personalize the topic you're discussing.

Or maybe you decide that, this week, the best thing you can do to love, influence and care for your few is to throw away all of your small group questions and play a game instead. Some of your best conversations might happen while you're playing basketball or going for a walk.

While activities might look different for every small group, remember you have the freedom to improvise. Because here's the good news—the point of your small group conversation isn't to make it through every discussion question. The point is to help your few engage in a conversation about authentic faith so they can better live out authentic faith. So if you want to better engage your few by scripting less and improvising more, **try an activity!**

SMALL GROUP SURVIVAL KIT: PENS & PAPER

This survival kit item might be the most important of all. When your conversation just isn't working well, hand out paper and pens to everyone! You can choose to use these however you think works best, but you might want to try asking them to write down their responses on paper and giving them back to you. Another option is that they could write down numbers 1 through 5, and circle the answer they choose. Or maybe they just need something to do with their hands while they talk, and doodling is the perfect solution.

3. FOLLOW RABBIT TRAILS

There will be weeks when everything seems to be going well. Your few are engaging in the conversation. The questions seem to be working. The conversation is moving.

And there will also be weeks when the conversation will take a turn you didn't expect. Maybe it's prompted by something someone said, or by what the group nearby just shouted, or by a text that just came in, or by absolutely nothing at all. No matter where the interruption comes from, it's true—more often than you'd probably like, your small group conversation will be derailed by a rabbit trail.

Rabbit trails are funny little things, and the good ones will stick with you long after that small group conversation has ended.

Maybe this sounds familiar:

"I never really thought about how Jesus actually died. Like,
He really died."
"Like the dead groundhog I saw on the way here!"
"I saw a dead chicken on the way here!"
"Did you know if you cut off a chicken's head, the body can
keep running?"
"We chicken-sat for our neighbors last year."
"Did you know chickens sometimes eat their own eggs?"
"My friend told me that chickens sometimes eat
each other."

If the rabbit trails that pop up in your small group are
about chickens . . . or the best burger place in town . . . or
the video they just saw on YouTube, it's okay to shut those
conversations down so you can keep things moving.

But *sometimes* . . . sometimes you'll come across a rabbit
trail that's actually worth following.

Maybe Reuben will ask a question.
Or Jamal will share something that's been happening
at school.
Or Zach will tell you his mom is sick.

Not every rabbit trail is worth following, but if the rabbit
trail you're dealing with . . .
is timely
is important
sparks their interest
. . . then pursue it.

Because if you want to better engage your few by scripting
less and improvising more, sometimes, you'll need to
follow the rabbit trail.

4. GO WITH YOUR GUT

Okay, maybe the idea of improvising makes you nervous.
Maybe you like—no, *love*—having a plan. Maybe you're

nervous about moving away from the plan your student pastor gives you. Maybe you're worried you don't have permission.

If that's you, here's something to keep in mind.

No one knows your few like you know your few. Not even your student pastor.

Week after week, you are the person who . . . connects with them, knows them, and engages with them. You know their lives, their worlds, their quirks, and their backgrounds.

And since you know your few so well, it's up to you to customize your small group conversations so they work for your small group. We can give you some ideas, and your student pastor can give you some helpful questions. But the truth is, it's up to you. If you're going to script less and learn to improvise more, you're going to have to trust your gut, experiment, and sometimes even fail. That's okay. Sometimes you learn more from failing than you do from succeeding. Don't be afraid of it.

No one can tell you exactly how to lead your small group. Only you can do that.

So trust yourself. Because if you want to better engage your few by scripting less and improvising more, you don't need an instruction manual. You need to go with your gut.

After you've prepared, connected, and gotten to know your few, if you want your small group conversations to matter more, you're going to have to engage them in a conversation.

But not just any conversation—a conversation about authentic faith. That's why it's so important you learn to **speak less and listen more, control less and lead more, script less and improvise more.**

Because before a teenager can ENGAGE in a *life* of authentic faith, he may need to ENGAGE in a *conversation* about authentic faith.

QUIZ:

HOW WELL DO YOU IMPROVISE WITH YOUR FEW?

Here's a few questions to see just how flexible you can be!

On a scale of one to breaking out in a vicious sweat, how uncomfortable are you with going off-script in a small group conversation?

Rolling with
the punches

Sweating and
hyperventilating

1   2   3   4   5

What are some small group questions that have totally bombed?

What's one way you've learned to improvise when your small group script isn't working?

Have you ever completely thrown away your script? What happened?

What's the best rabbit trail you've ever followed?

NEXT STEP

The art of IMPROVISING looks different for everyone. Below, write one or two specific and practical tricks you can use to IMPROVISE when you need to shift your group conversation.

5

chapter
five
move

Move

Congratulations! You did it! You successfully engaged your small group of teenage guys in a conversation about authentic faith!

Well, not really. You're reading a book right now. You're not leading a small group.

But let's *pretend* you've been leading a successful conversation with your small group.

And now let's imagine you're ready to wrap up that conversation.

Sure, you could wrap things up by yelling, "Okay, we're done, bye!" and sprinting for the door.

But we know you. We know you care about making your small group conversations matter more. In fact, we're pretty sure you care so much about making them matter that you wouldn't just throw it all away in the last few moments of your time together. You're going to be strategic. You're going to finish strong.

Because it's great to engage your few in a conversation about authentic faith, but leading small group conversations isn't the only reason you signed up to be a small group leader, is it? You signed up to be a small group leader because you wanted . . .
to make a big difference.
to change the world.

to invest in a few teenage guys so you could help them develop a lifelong, authentic kind of faith.

That's why we know you won't wrap up your small group conversation by lunging for the door.

Once you've engaged your few in a *conversation* about authentic faith, your final step is to **move your few to engage in a life of authentic faith.** In other words, after you've engaged them inside your circle, it's your job to move them to engage outside your circle.

So before you move for the door, here are three ways to keep your few moving toward authentic faith—even after the conversation has ended.

If you want to move your few, GIVE a next step.

When we talked about leading—not *controlling*—your small group conversations, we talked about the importance of keeping the end in mind. Your ultimate . . .
destination
target
finish-line
goal
. . . isn't necessarily to help your few remember what they've heard. As their small group leader, your goal is to help them *apply* it.

Keep that goal in mind as you wrap up your small group conversation each week. Before you move your few out of your circle and back into the world, give them a next step. When you help them identify one simple step they can take during the week, you'll help your few learn to not only *talk* about their faith but to *live* it out, too. So wrap up your conversation each week by asking, "What's one thing you're going to do this week to live this out?"

Then be sure to follow up. In an individual or group text, ask them how it's going or remind them of how they can live out what they're learning. Not only is it a great reminder, but your few will become used to the idea that what they're learning at church is meant to carry over into the rest of the week.

Remember, when you give a next step, you move them toward action.

If you want to move your few, PRAY together.

You may not always have time in small group to hear from every guy about every prayer request he's ever had, but you do have time to close in prayer. Some weeks, everyone might have the opportunity to pray. Other weeks, you may only have time for one. But whether you have ten minutes or ten seconds for prayer, don't forget to pray together.

Get in the habit of asking your few for prayer requests.
Then write down their prayer requests.
And follow up on their prayer requests.

When you pray for, and with, your few, you're modeling what it looks like to talk to God, to know God and to trust God. Imagine the impact you could have on a teenage guy's faith if your weekly small group conversations helped him have better conversations, not just with his small group, but with the God who made him.

Did you know that there is research that shows us that prayer strengthens the part of our brain that helps us understand the concept of a loving God? By praying together, you're not just transitioning to the end of your group time, you're helping your few grow in their understanding of their loving heavenly Father.

When you pray together, you move them toward God.

You've heard the statistics on public speaking, right? I'm not sure if people really are more afraid to speak in public than die, but I sure know that most teenage guys don't love the idea of praying out loud. But as small group leaders, I think we can ease them into getting more and more comfortable with this as they get older.

Here are a few things that I (Brett) would try with my group to get them more comfortable with praying out loud:

1. Change the posture. I get it, holding hands in a circle isn't something most groups will be comfortable with. But do something to change the position of where they've been for group. The physical change will help with a mental, emotional, and spiritual change. I've found it works well to have the group stand, circle up, and grab the shoulder of the guy next to them.

2. Try being thankful. End small group by going around the circle and asking your few one thing they're thankful for. You, as the SGL, can start, guide it around the circle, and when it gets back to you, say, "Amen." Show them prayer can be different than they're used to (and be okay when they say they're grateful for girls, spring break, or that a certain team lost the previous day).

3. Keep it casual. The more natural, authentic, and concise your prayers are, the better you'll model what it can look like for them to do the same.

Sometimes we're tempted to skim over prayer time because it can be awkward or even frustrating, or we're just out of time. But just like anything else, prayer is something we get better at with practice. It also is something that becomes easier the more we do it. So, if you want your few to move, **PRAY** together.

Finally,

If you want to move your few, SAY something meaningful.

If you've led well, you've probably spent most of your small group conversation asking questions, listening, and asking more questions. But as your small group conversation comes to a close, and your few are preparing to leave the safe place of your small group for another week, you have the opportunity to say something meaningful—something that has the potential to stay with them all week long.

Like . . .
"I love you, guys."
"I'm praying for you."
"I'm proud of you."
"I'm here for you."
"I believe in you."

When you say something meaningful to your few, you help them to feel significant. Who knows the impact those words might have on even one teenage guy in your group. Every bit of encouragement counts. After all, a few words can make a big difference in the direction of someone's life. When you take your time at the end of group, you are showing them that no matter what they did or said in group, you still love them and you're still for them. And that means they're more likely to come back and engage next week.

So before you move your few out of your circle, choose your words wisely. Say something meaningful. When you do, you'll move them toward feeling as significant as you already know they are.

If you want to move your few, MOVE WITH THEM.

We get it. You're a busy person, and after your group
conversation is over you have . . .
a dinner to microwave.
a spouse to see.
a roommate to chat with.
a day job to prep for.
But before you bolt for your car, make sure you don't miss
a huge opportunity. The few minutes after group are one of
the most strategic times to connect with individual guys in
your group. Maybe you need to . . .
follow up on one of his answers during group.
clarify what he meant when he said something surprising.
clarify something you meant when it came out differently
than you intended.
encourage him.
ask about his mom or his math test or his cat.

As you wrap up your small group conversation, remember
to finish strong. When you give a next step, pray together,
say something meaningful, and walk out with them, you
help your few move—not just out of your circle, but into a
life of more authentic faith.

Imagine.

If you are a middle school small group leader, you have
about 150 small groups over the course of the three years
of middle school.

If you are a high school small group leader, you have
about 200 small groups over the course of the four years
of high school.

You can make every single one of them count.
And you can make every single one of them matter.
And just like every individual conversation, they'll all go
better if you start with the end in mind.

Just imagine . . .

Three years from now, your quirky sixth grade guy will walk into the world of high school. In a whole new world, exposed to pressures and experiences he has only seen in movies. He'll face challenges that he couldn't have imagined back in sixth grade. And he'll be ready because he took with him 150 conversations that gave him wisdom, encouragement, and beliefs.

Four years from now, your somewhat mature ninth grade guy will walk through whatever is next. In a whole new world without mom or dad or your church, he'll face challenges that he couldn't have imagined back in ninth grade. And he'll be ready because he took with him 200 conversations that gave him wisdom, belonging, and faith.

When he feels lost, your group memories may just push him to find friends who share his faith.

When he encounters doubts, he may just call someone in your group because it's always been a safe place to ask tough questions.

And when he stands in all the noise of high school, college, or life in general there's a good chance he'll still hear YOUR voice in the back of his mind reminding him to . . .
make the wise choice
put others first
trust God
find community
or pray.

Your conversation this week matters.

And it can MATTER MORE in light of all those conversations over time.

conclusion

Conclusion

So if you want to have better conversations with the teenage guys in your small group . . .
PREPARE for the conversation you'll have in your circle.
CONNECT with your few, and help them connect with each other.
KNOW your few, and help them know each other.
ENGAGE your few by speaking less, listening more, controlling less, leading more, scripting less and improvising more.
MOVE your few toward a life of authentic faith outside your circle.

That's not easy. Leading conversations with teenage guys can still be difficult, no matter how well you prepare, connect, know, engage, or move your few. Sometimes . . .
they'll still be distracted.
you'll still ask a question that bombs.
they'll still sit in silence.
you'll still lose control.
they'll still ask questions you can't answer.
you'll still wonder who put you in charge.

Group talk isn't a science, it's an art.

And you were made in the image of the greatest Artist.
That means . . .
you were made to create.
you were made to design.
you were made to express.

You are an artist.

You get it from Him.

We probably haven't answered all of your questions.
We probably haven't solved all of your problems.
But we hope we've shared at least a few stories, ideas, and strategies that will help you make your next small group conversation a little more effective.

So this week . . .
Prepare
Connect
Know
Engage
Move.

And remember . . .

Every conversation with your small group MATTERS. But you can make this week's conversation MATTER EVEN MORE.

author
bios

Author bios

JEREMY ZACH

Jeremy, or "JZ," spent 10 years as a paid, professional youth pastor in the local church. He received a BA in Communication Studies from University of Minnesota and my MDIV (Masters of Divinity) from Fuller Theological Seminary in Pasadena. Jeremy is the father of two girls, Harlow and Aria, and two calico cats. A few things that he enjoys are hot, hot sauce, YouTube cat videos, and loud EDM music.

TOM SHEFCHUNAS

Tom Shefchunas, or "Shef" as most people call him, has worked with students for over 20 years. He has been a teacher, a coach, a high school principal, and a father. Before joining Orange as the Executive Director of Student Strategy, Tom was North Point Ministries' Multi-Campus Director of Transit for 12 years. He has an undergraduate degree in Physics, and graduate degrees in both Educational Leadership and Biblical Studies. He and his wife, Julie, have three children.

BRETT TALLEY

Brett Talley is an XP3 Orange Specialist with Orange after 11 years in full time ministry. He's been married to his amazing wife since 2004. They have three awesome and hilarious kids who constantly keep them busy and laughing. He loves baseball, golf, and makes amazing turkey melt sandwiches (if he has the time and ingredients, otherwise they're just average). Connect with Brett on Twitter & Instagram @brettryantalley for pictures of the cutest kids in the world.

LEARN MORE
ABOUT LEAD SMALL
+
DOWNLOAD OUR
UBERCOOL AMAZING
FREE APP
@ LEADSMALL.ORG